LET'S EXPLORE SCIENCE

ROCKS, MINERALS, and soil

AUTHOR
SUSAN
MARKOWITZ
MEREDITH

Rourke
Educational Media
rourkeeducationalmedia.com

www.rourkeeducationalmedia.com

PHOTO CREDITS: © Lukasz Witczak, Achim Prill, Andrejs Zemdega: Title Page; © Plus: 4; © David Hardman: 4; © Matthias Straka: 5; © ranplett: 6; © Ashok Rodrigues: 6; © George Clerk: 6; © ugurhan betin: 7; © Robyn MacKenzie: 8; © Sean Curry: 8, 16; © Dragon Trifunovic: 9, 25; © Tobias Helbig: 10; © Lisa Thornberg: 11; © Vinicius Ramalho Tupinamba: 11; © DNY59: 11; © Katherine Moffitt: 12; © Rob Belknap: 12; © Melissa Carroll: 12, 19, 21, 23, 26, 27; © JulienGrondin: 13, 41; © Korsakova Liudmila: 14, 23; © Paige Falk: 15; © Aquacolor: 16; © Iain McGillivray: 16; © Stephan Morris: 18; © NASA: 19; © Sandra vom Stein: 20; © morganl: 21; © Richard Simpkins: 21, 23; © mikeuk: 21; © Guy Sargent: 21, 23; © Dmitry Demidovich 22; © P_Wei: 23; © sabrina dei nobili: 23; © David Woods: 23; © ideeone: 24; © Rainer Walter Schmied: 26; © Mark Rasmussen: 26; © Karol Kozlowski: 28; © Melissa Carroll: 28 (top); © Jonathan Winney: 29; © Skip ODonnell: 29; © Paula Connelly: 29; © Marcus Lindstrom: 29; © Andraz Cerar: 29; © Arpad Benedek: 30; © ChrisCrowley: 30; © Miroslava Holasová: 30; © only_fabrizio: 30; © Wikipedia: 30; © Igor_Kali: 30; © Bonnie Jacobs: 31; © Martin Bowker: 32; © Grigory Bibikov: 33; © Brian Prawl: 33; © Valeria Titova: 33; © Clayton Hansen: 34; © Serghia Velusceac: 35; © Alasdair Thomson: 35; © Hui Yee Yeap: 36; © Amanda Rohde: 37; © Malcolm Romain: 38; © asterix0597: 42; © johnnyscriv: 43

Edited by Kelli Hicks

Cover design by Teri Intzegian

Interior designed by Tara Raymo

Library of Congress Cataloging-in-Publication Data

Meredith, Susan, 1951-
  Rocks, minerals, and soil / Susan Meredith.
    p. cm. -- (Let's explore science)
  Includes index.
  ISBN 978-1-60694-411-0 (hard cover)
  ISBN 978-1-60694-529-2 (soft cover)
  1. Rocks--Juvenile literature. 2. Minerals--Juvenile literature. 3. Soils--Juvenile literature. I. Title.
  QE432.2.M47 2010
  552--dc22
                        2009008948

Printed in China, FOFO I - Production Company
  Shenzhen, Guangdong Province

Rourke
Educational Media

rourkeeducationalmedia.com

customerservice@rourkeeducationalmedia.com • PO Box 643328 Vero Beach, Florida 32964

Table of Contents

Chapter One

Earth's Ingredients

Rocks, minerals, and soil make up our solid Earth. We depend on them everyday. We use rocks, for instance, in all of our streets and highways. Our homes and buildings also contain rock, both inside and out.

Minerals play a big role in our lives, too. Coins and cell phones, computers and glass, all make use of minerals. Wires that carry electricity to our cities and towns contain minerals as well. So do pencils and toothpaste.

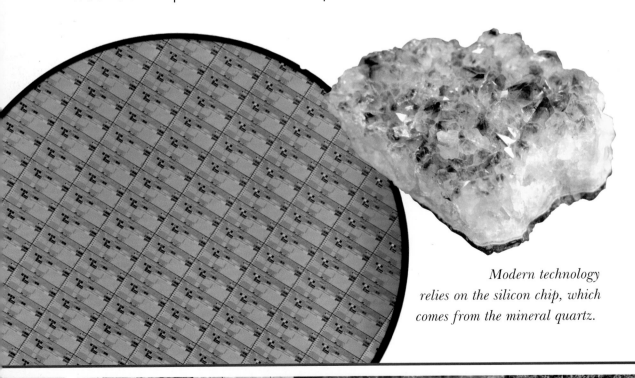

Modern technology relies on the silicon chip, which comes from the mineral quartz.

Our dependency on soil is just as great. Soil is the very ground under our feet. We walk and build on it. We also grow plants in it. Whether it's farmland, prairie, or forest, the plants of the world need soil. The rest of us need plants to survive.

MINERAL

ROCK

SOIL

Rocks, minerals, and soil are all useful to us in their own ways. But they are not as separate as they seem. These materials are linked together throughout nature.

Rock Basics

Rock is the hard, solid material all around us. Huge masses of rock make up the solid part of Earth. But rocks come in smaller sizes, too—from boulders and pebbles to sand and clay.

BOULDERS

SAND

PEBBLES

Whatever their size, rocks share something in common; they all consist of minerals. Most rocks contain two or more minerals. Sometimes, though, a single mineral makes up a rock. Minerals in many rocks are easy to see. But minerals can be very tiny as well.

People often mine rocks for the minerals they contain.

Minerals; Unique in Structure and Make-up

Minerals are chemical substances commonly found on Earth. There are thousands of known minerals. However, only about 25 make up most types of rock.

Each mineral, whatever its location, has a specific chemical make-up. Its ingredients include **elements,** the most basic chemicals found in all matter. Minerals consist of one or more elements.

Minerals fit into seven main groups based on their chemical make-up.

Amateur geologists collect mineral samples like this Galena for their beautiful colors and interesting crystal shapes.

Every mineral also has a unique structure. It stays the same whatever the mineral's size. This three-dimensional shape comes from the mineral's elements. Each one has its own building blocks, called **atoms.** When elements combine in a mineral, their atoms arrange themselves in a specific way.

The atoms in some minerals arrange themselves in an orderly pattern. These minerals take form as **crystals.** A crystal is a solid with many repeating flat surfaces. Minerals that do not form crystals grow in a less orderly way. Their atoms have a less orderly arrangement, too.

Rocks and Minerals Make Different Soils

Soil is loose material found on the Earth's surface. It consists mostly of rock and mineral particles. But soil also contains the remains of plant and animal life, known as organic matter.

A top layer of soil covers most of the Earth's land. Soil also forms under rivers, lakes, and oceans.

There are many different kinds of soil. Their look and feel often varies from place to place. The soil's rock and mineral particles play a big role in those differences. Factors such as particle size and chemical make-up affect the soil.

Chapter Two

Three Types of Rock

Rocks may be speckled or solid-colored, bumpy or smooth, dense or filled with holes. A rock's look has a lot to do with its mineral make-up. But, just as important is how the rock formed. There are three types of rock formations. One type forms when melted rock cools and hardens. A second type consists of layers of small particles. The third rock type forms under intense heat and pressure.

How Are They Formed?

Granite forms when melted rock cools and hardens.

Layers of small particles created this rock commonly known as coal.

Intense heat and pressure caused this rock, called marble, to form.

Rock Formed by Cooling and Hardening

One type of rock gets its start deep in the Earth in huge underground pockets. There, the rock is so hot that it melts. This molten rock, called **magma,** is like a soup of different minerals and elements.

Because magma is less dense (and lighter in weight) than the solid rock around it, it flows upward. As it rises to the surface, Earth's temperature gets lower. The magma cools and hardens. The result is **igneous** rock.

Magma's temperature is 1400° to 2300 °F (760° to 1300 °C).

Igneous Rock Below Ground

Magma often flows up through deep cracks in the solid rock already there. Sometimes it spreads out between layers of older rock. Sometimes it cuts across different layers, pushing against the rock as it moves. This magma eventually settles below ground to cool and harden.

Underground, or **intrusive,** igneous rock forms very slowly. It cools and hardens over tens of thousands of years. During this period, the rock's minerals have a long time to form crystals, or crystallize. Often these crystals grow large enough to see.

Granite is an example of an intrusive igneous rock.

This huge granite rock in Yosemite National Park rises more than 4,737 feet (1,444 meters) above the valley floor.

Igneous Rock Above Ground

Hot magma also rises to the Earth's surface. It often pushes up through long, open pipelines in solid rock. These cone-like mountains, called volcanoes, build up in size as more and more magma flows out.

When magma meets the air and hardens, it forms **extrusive** igneous rock. It hardens very quickly. In other words, all of its minerals crystallize rapidly. As a result, they are very small.

OBSIDIAN

PUMICE

BASALT

LAVA FLOW

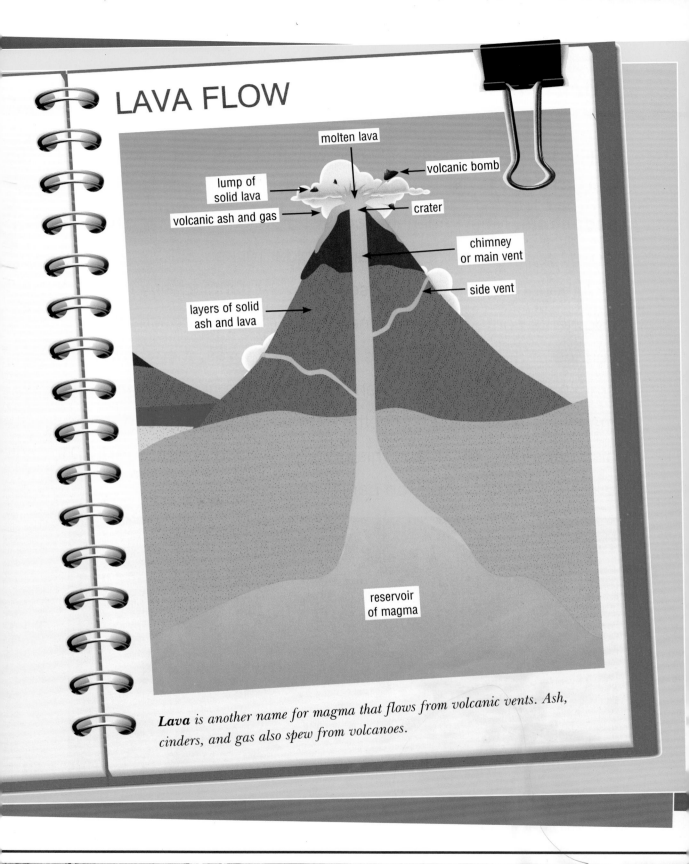

molten lava

volcanic bomb

lump of solid lava

crater

volcanic ash and gas

chimney or main vent

side vent

layers of solid ash and lava

reservoir of magma

Lava is another name for magma that flows from volcanic vents. Ash, cinders, and gas also spew from volcanoes.

Rock Formed From Particles

Hardening magma is only one way that rock forms. A second type of rock forms from layers of small particles, called **sediments.** Most sediments consist of tiny bits of rock. The loose fragments come from larger, older rocks.

Although solid rocks may seem never-changing, tiny rock fragments come off all the time. Sometimes rain loosens the surface of a rock. Sometimes water that freezes, then thaws, cracks open rocks and loosens particles. The tiny fragments may fall down slopes and settle. Running water and wind may also carry particles away. This process, known as **weathering,** takes place everywhere on Earth.

Over millions of years, rivers can create canyons by eroding layer upon layer of rock.

These particles may be carried great distances. They may end up in a sea, a lakebed, or even on dry land. There, the sediments settle layer after layer.

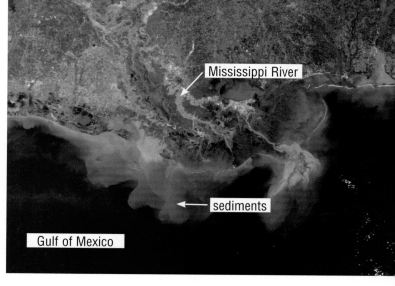

Everyday, the Mississippi River deposits thousands of tons of sediments when it reaches the Gulf of Mexico.

Other Sediments

Sediments also come from other sources, such as organic matter. In seawater, countless tiny shells and skeletons may form layers on the bottom. In swamps, decaying plants slowly build up.

Certain minerals dissolved in a body of water can form sediments, too. The process starts as the water slowly

evaporates. Over time, less and less water remains to mix with the minerals. The excess minerals start grouping together to form crystals. These crystals slowly build up.

Evaporation caused Gypsum like this to crystallize in large, thick mineral beds.

Layers Squeezed Together

Whatever the sediment, its deposits form thousands upon thousands of layers. As new layers settle on top, they bury lower layers deeper down in the earth. The weight of the upper layers squeezes the lower layers together. Moisture in the deepest layers causes certain minerals to grow. As they do, they cement all the sediments together. The result is **sedimentary** rock. The process takes hundreds of thousands of years.

The Wave is a sandstone formation on the slopes of Arizona's Coyote Buttes.

Sedimentary rock from rock fragments:

sandstone (sand)

shale (clay and mud)

conglomerate sedimentary rock (mix of pebbles with mud or sand)

Sedimentary rock from organic matter:

limestone (shells and bones)

coal (fossilized remains of swamp plants)

Sedimentary rock from dissolved minerals:

halite (edible "rock salt")

Rock Formed By Heat and Pressure

A third type of rock forms when heat and/or pressure change old, solid rock. This happens far below Earth's surface. There, extreme conditions may cause a rock's minerals to break apart and form new crystals. Or, various minerals in the rock may come together to form new minerals. **Metamorphic** rock is the result of this process.

Sometimes gases are present when metamorphic rock forms. These gases may add new elements to combine with the rock's minerals. Their interaction can create new minerals.

Often huge masses of deeply buried rock change into metamorphic rock. But small areas can change, too. This happens when flowing magma touches the solid rock around it. The intense heat causes the old rock's minerals to re-crystallize.

Buried Rock

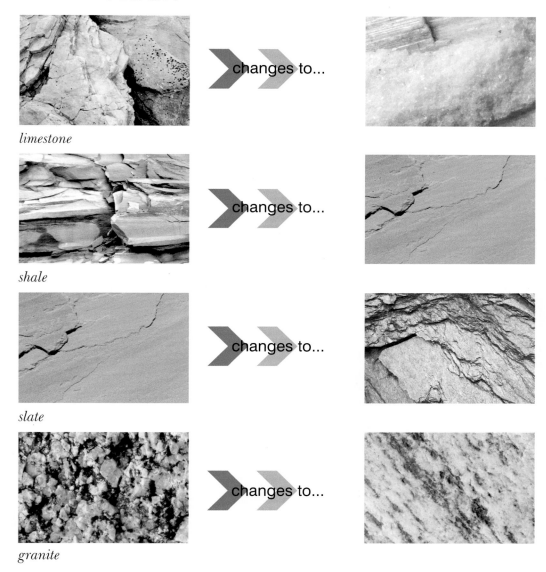

limestone   changes to...

shale   changes to...

slate   changes to...

granite   changes to...

Chapter Three

Looking at Minerals

Rocks form as their minerals grow. Each mineral begins to build its solid shape at a certain temperature. Most minerals need liquid in order to grow. Different minerals grow at different rates.

Various gases, liquids, and other minerals can affect the way a mineral grows.

As they grow, minerals take various forms. Many minerals form crystals. But others form into grains, fibers, or nuggets—even irregular chunks. Still, others grow into several different forms. Each of those forms developed under different conditions.

A mineral's habit is its most common form.

Crystal Shapes

For a mineral to form a crystal, it needs room to grow. With enough space, crystals grow in groups to produce larger crystalline structures. But not all crystals have the same pattern of flat surfaces. Some crystals have the shape of cubes. Others look like flat boxes or rectangles on end. Still, others have the shape of six-sided boxes. Minerals occur in a variety of crystal shapes.

EXAMPLES OF CRYSTAL SHAPES

MONOCLINIC

CUBIC

HEXAGONAL

ORTHORHOMBIC

TETRAGONAL

TRICLINIC

Turquoise

Perhaps the most beautiful crystals of all are gemstones. They form only under certain conditions. The common mineral **corundum**, for instance, has no color. But trace amounts of different elements may occasionally tint the corundum. Rubies and sapphires are both colorful forms of corundum.

Other Properties of Minerals

Minerals vary in other ways, too, including how they split apart. Some minerals break into irregular chunks. Other minerals tend to split into thin sheets. Still, others split into cube shapes. These various shapes relate directly to the arrangement of atoms in the mineral.

Like many other minerals, mica splits into flat surfaces called cleavages.

Outside color is another property that identifies many minerals. But it doesn't work every time. Sometimes a mineral occurs in several different colors. When that happens, the best way to identify the mineral is to look at its **streak.** A streak is the powder left behind when the mineral rubs across a dull-white surface. A mineral's streak will always have the same color, even if its outside colors are different.

Hematite often looks black, but the streak it produces is always reddish brown.

Every mineral also has a certain shine, or luster. A mineral's chemical make-up determines its luster. Some minerals have a metallic shine because they contain metal elements. Many other minerals are nonmetallic. They may look glassy, silky, pearly, or even dull.

PLATINUM

GOLD

COPPER

MERCURY

ALUMINUM

Metal elements include gold, silver, iron, copper, lead, mercury, uranium, zinc, platinum, and aluminum.

Minerals differ in their hardness, too. A fingernail can make scratches in some minerals. But even a knife cannot scratch other minerals. Diamonds are so hard that nothing on Earth can scratch them.

Moh's Scale

In 1822, Friedrich Mohs of Germany created a scale to measure the hardness of all minerals. This scale remains in use today.

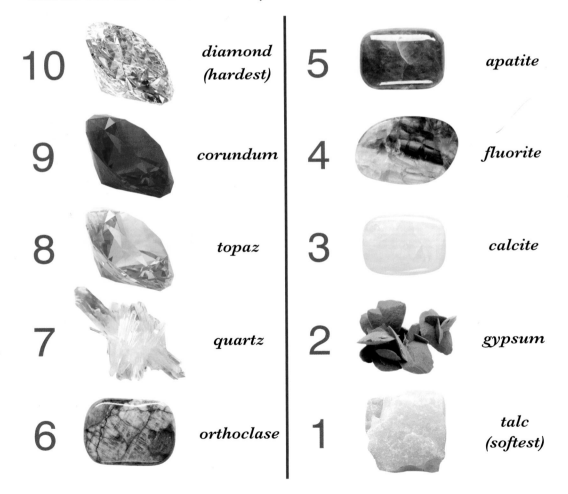

10		*diamond (hardest)*	5	*apatite*
9		*corundum*	4	*fluorite*
8		*topaz*	3	*calcite*
7		*quartz*	2	*gypsum*
6		*orthoclase*	1	*talc (softest)*

A sample mineral that scratches calcite (#3) but not fluorite (#4) has a hardness of 3.

Identifying a mineral requires a close look at its different properties. But some minerals are easier to identify because they have a unique quality. Halite, for instance, tastes salty. The soft mineral talc feels greasy. Kaolin, another mineral, smells like freshly plowed soil.

Chapter Four

Soil Formation

Soil gets its start when rocks break down. Little by little, the forces of wind and water, heat and cold, loosen rock surfaces. In time, bits of rocks and minerals break free. These particles slowly build up. Beneath them is the rock from which they came, also known as parent material.

Sometimes wind and water carry rock particles to a new location where the parent material is different.

CLAY　　**SILT**　　**SAND**

Rock particles in soil may be large, small, or in between. Some soils contain gravel and pebbles, while others are sandy. Still, others have particles known as silt, which is less coarse than sand. The finest particles in soil are clay. Many soils are a mix of clay, silt, and sand.

Life in the Soil

In order to form, soil also needs organic matter. This matter comes from decaying plants and animals. Tiny grazers, such as ants, beetles, and slugs feed on these remains. In so doing, they help break them down into smaller bits. Bacteria and other micro-organisms break down the organic matter even more.

Decaying organic matter, called **humus** helps make soil. Bit by bit, the humus helps separate rock particles. In so doing, it allows more water and air to enter the soil, and stay there. Air and water are important ingredients in soil, too.

Earthworms are like tiny plows. They turn over soil as they dig through it. In the process, they break up tightly packed particles.

Humus helps the soil to support plant life.

Soils Form Differently

Soil develops very slowly. It may take thousands of years to form. Even so, more soil forms in some areas than others. One important reason is the climate of an area. If a region is hot and humid, for instance, rock surfaces loosen more quickly. Organic matter breaks down faster, too. This produces more soil.

The specific location also influences how soil forms. On a steep slope, for example, water may carry away soil particles. Melting snow may wash soil away, too. New soil often collects in valleys.

The kinds of rock and mineral particles in a soil affect its formation.

There are many different soil colors—from yellowish and red to dark brown and gray.

Layers of Soil

As soil develops, different layers appear. Over time, most soil forms into three layers called soil horizons. Each one may be thin or thick.

The top layer, or A horizon, has more humus than the others. It is deep enough to support plant roots. The middle layer, or B horizon, has less organic material than the top layer. But it contains many minerals. Below this layer is the C horizon, which looks more like the parent material.

SOIL LAYERS

A Horizon
called topsoil

B Horizon
called subsoil

C Horizon
called soil material

Chapter Five

The Changing Earth

Rocks, minerals, and soil are always on the move. They are constantly combining, and recombining. These changes take place both above and below the Earth's surface.

The Rock Cycle

The oldest and slowest Earth cycle is rock formation. From deep in the Earth, hot magma rises up. The magma cools and hardens into igneous rock. Over time, weathering forces loosen its surface and carry away rock and mineral fragments. These fragments build up in layers. Eventually the layers cement into sedimentary rock. Its deepest layers face so much pressure and heat that they change into metamorphic rock. When this rock gets hot enough, it melts back into magma. And so the cycle begins again.

ROCK CYCLE

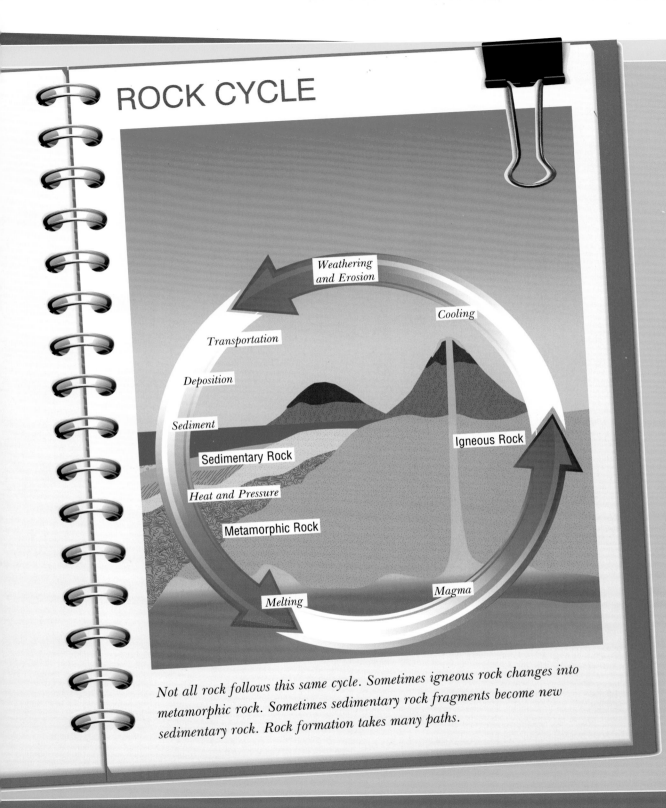

Weathering and Erosion

Cooling

Transportation

Deposition

Sediment

Sedimentary Rock

Heat and Pressure

Metamorphic Rock

Igneous Rock

Melting

Magma

Not all rock follows this same cycle. Sometimes igneous rock changes into metamorphic rock. Sometimes sedimentary rock fragments become new sedimentary rock. Rock formation takes many paths.

Many rock and mineral fragments have an extended stay on the Earth's surface. They become soil particles. In fact, soil gets a fresh supply of rock and mineral fragments all the time. Living organisms also provide the soil with organic matter on a regular basis.

But soil gets lost, too. Natural forces remove soil from an area, at times very quickly. Human activities also destroy soil in different ways. For instance, our buildings and roads sometimes cover over fertile soil. Certain farming techniques harm the soil, too. These methods cause soil nutrients to drain away.

Protect Resources

Rocks, minerals, and soil are important natural resources. Our society makes use of them daily. We crush huge masses of rock for building materials. We dig mines the world over in search of minerals. And we grow crops on millions of acres of farmland.

These valuable resources are here for the taking. But it's up to us to use them wisely.

Helping to Protect Our Resources

Glossary

atoms (AT-uhms): the tiniest parts, or building blocks, of elements

corundum (ko-RUN-duhm): a common, colorless mineral that occasionally occurs in gemstone form

crystals (KRISS-tuhls): the solid forms of a substance, such as a mineral, containing many repeated flat surfaces

elements (EL-uh-muhnts): basic chemicals found in all matter that cannot be split into simpler substances

extrusive (ex-TRUH-siv): igneous rock that forms above ground

humus (HYOO-muhss): decaying organic matter in the soil

igneous (IG-nee-uhss): a type of rock formed when rising magma cools and hardens

intrusive (in-TRUH-siv): igneous rock that forms below ground

lava (LAH-va): magma that flows out of a volcano

magma (MAG-muh): hot, liquid rock often found deep beneath the Earth's surface in underground pockets

metamorphic (met-uh-MOR-fik): a type of rock that is created when pre-existing rock changes form due to heat and/or pressure

sediments (SED-uh-ments): particles of rock and other materials that settle, often in layers

sedimentary (sed-uh-MEN-tuh-ree): a type of rock formed by layers that are squeezed and cemented together

streak (STREEK): a long, thin smear, often referring to the powder left behind when the mineral rubs across a dull-white surface

weathering (WETH-ur-eeng): changes caused by natural forces, including rain, ice, and wind

Index

Websites to visit

terraweb.wr.usgs.gov/TRS/kids
www.mnh.si.edu/earth/main_frames.html
www.fi.edu/fellows/fellow1/oct98/create
www.minsocam.org/MSA/K12/K_12.html
www.rocksforkids.com/RFK/identification.html

About the author

Susan Markowitz Meredith likes to learn about the nature of things. She especially enjoys sharing what she discovers with young readers. So far, she has written 40 books on a variety of topics, including natural science. Ms. Meredith also has produced quite a few TV shows for young thinkers.